A Benjamin Blog and his Inquisitive Dog Investigation

Exploring Coral Reefs

Anita Ganeri

Heinemann
LIBRARY

Chicago, Illinois

© 2014 Heinemann Library
an imprint of Capstone Global Library, LLC
Chicago, Illinois

To contact Capstone Global Library please
phone 800-747-4992, or visit our web site,
www.capstonepub.com

Edited by Dan Nunn, Rebecca Rissman, and Helen
Cox Cannons
Designed by Joanna Hinton-Malivoire
Original illustrations © Capstone Global Library Ltd
Illustrated by Sernur ISIK
Picture research by Mica Brancic
Production by Helen McCreath
Originated by Capstone Global Library Ltd

**Library of Congress Cataloging-in-Publication
Data**
Ganeri, Anita, 1961- author.
   Exploring coral reefs : a Benjamin Blog and his
inquisitive dog investigation / Anita Ganeri.
       pages cm.—(Exploring habitats, with Benjamin
Blog and his inquisitive dog)
   Includes bibliographical references and index.
   ISBN 978-1-4329-8780-0 (hb)—ISBN 978-1-4329-
8787-9 (pb) 1. Coral reef ecology—Juvenile
literature. 2. Coral reefs and islands—Juvenile
literature. 3. Coral reef animals—Juvenile literature.
I. Title.

QH541.5.C7G36 2014
551.42'4—dc23   2013017421

Acknowledgments
The author and publisher are grateful to the
following for permission to reproduce copyright
material: FLPA pp. 16 (Imagebroker), 18
(OceanPhoto); Getty Images p. 9 (Lonely Planet
Images/James Lyon); Photoshot p. 24 (© NHPA/
Michael Patrick O'Neill); Reuters p. 26 (© Ho
New); Shutterstock pp 4 (© VVO), 5 (© Richard
Whitcombe), 6 (© Tyler Fox), 7 (© Pinosub), 8
(© tororo reaction), 10 (© Rich Carey), 11 (© R
Gombarik), 12 (© Brian Kinney), 13 (© Krzysztof
Odziomek), 14 (© stephan kerkhofs), 15 (©
Sergey Skleznev), 17 (© Rich Carey), 19 (© Brian
Kinney), 20 (© James A Dawson), 21 (© Olga
Khoroshunova), 22 (© Ingvars Birznieks),
23 (© Kristina Vackova), 25 (© tororo reaction), 27
(© tae208), 29 top (© Rich Carey), 29 bottom
(© tae208).

Cover photograph of Vanua Levu Barrier Reef, Fiji,
in the Pacific Ocean, reproduced with permission
of Getty Images (Lonely Planet Images/Casey
Mahaney).

We would like to thank Michael Bright for his
invaluable help in the preparation of this book.

Some words are shown in bold, **like this**. You can find
out what they mean by looking in the glossary.

Contents

Welcome to Coral Reefs!

Hello! My name's Benjamin Blog and this is Barko Polo, my **inquisitive** dog. (He's named after the ancient ace explorer **Marco Polo**.) We have just returned from our latest adventure—exploring **coral reefs** around the world. We put this book together from some of the blog posts we wrote on the way.

BARKO'S BLOG-TASTIC CORAL REEF FACTS

Coral reefs are the richest **habitats** in the ocean. They are home to thousands of creatures, from clown fish and porcupine fish, to giant clams, sea cucumbers, and sharks.

Coral Builders

Coral reefs are amazing places, and I couldn't wait to dive in. First, I wanted to find out how reefs are made. They are built by millions of tiny sea creatures, called coral **polyps**. The polyps grow hard cases around their bodies. When they die, the cases are left behind.

BARKO'S BLOG-TASTIC CORAL REEF FACTS

Coral polyps belong to the same family as sea anemones. Like sea anemones, polyps have stinging **tentacles**. They wave their tentacles in the water to catch tiny creatures to eat.

7

Ready, Steady, Grow

Posted by: Ben Blog | July 11 at 2:45 p.m.

Tropical coral reefs grow along the coast in tropical oceans. They like warm, clean, shallow water—that's fine for me, too! Tiny plants, called **algae**, live inside some polyps' bodies and help the **polyps** make their hard cases. The algae need plenty of sunlight to make their own food.

BARKO'S BLOG-TASTIC CORAL REEF FACTS

Atolls, like this one, are tiny **coral** islands. They start as reefs growing around volcanoes that poked up from the ocean floor. Slowly, the volcanoes sink, leaving the atolls behind.

Daisies, Mushrooms, and Brains

Posted by: Ben Blog | August 18 at 7:52 p.m.

I've reached the main part of the reef and counted 10 types of **coral** already. There are many different sizes and shapes. There are corals that look like daisies, mushrooms, and deer antlers. This is brain coral. It can grow to 6½ feet (2 meters) across. Can you guess how it got its name?

BARKO'S BLOG-TASTIC CORAL REEF FACTS

When coral is alive, it's brightly colored—pink, blue, purple, yellow, and green. Dead coral is chalky white.

Fabulous Fish

Posted by: Ben Blog | September 3 at 11:25 a.m.

It's daytime on the reef, and there are fabulous fish everywhere. In fact, more types of fish make their home on **coral reefs** than anywhere else in the ocean. I took this photo of a **school** of butterfly fish. Their bright colors help them spot each other in the crowd.

BARKO'S BLOG-TASTIC CORAL REEF FACTS
The parrot fish gets its name from its sharp, beak-like teeth. Its beak is perfect for crunching on coral and scraping **algae** from the rocks to eat.

beak

Coral reefs are crowded places, so fish and other creatures take turns to feed. Some fish come out in the daytime. Other fish come out at night. In the day, these soldierfish hide in holes in the **coral**. At night, they use their large eyes to find food in the dark.

BARKO'S BLOG-TASTIC CORAL REEF FACTS

If a **predator** tries to attack a lionfish, it's in for a painful surprise. The lionfish's feathery fins are covered in poisonous spines that it jabs into its enemy. Ouch!

Night Hunters

Tonight we went on another night dive. This time, I was searching for sharks. Whitetip reef sharks are expert hunters. They can sniff out fish hiding in cracks in the **coral** and wriggle inside to get them out. They can also pick up tiny bleeps of electricity that fish give out when they swim.

BARKO'S BLOG-TASTIC CORAL REEF FACTS

A moray eel hides in its hole, with just its head poking out. Its mouth is lined with large, razor-sharp teeth for catching any passing fish, squid, and crabs.

Danger lurks around every corner on a **coral reef**. Some reef creatures have special ways of staying alive. Stonefish sit on the ocean floor. They look like weed-covered rocks. But they also have sharp spines on their back for shooting deadly venom, or liquid poison, into their enemies.

sharp spine

BARKO'S BLOG-TASTIC CORAL REEF FACTS
Surgeonfish have two sharp, spike-like spines on either side of their tail. If a fish is attacked, its spines stick out and it swipes its tail from side to side.

Living Together

Posted by: Ben Blog | December 5 at 12:36 p.m.

Back in the water, I'm watching a moray eel getting its teeth cleaned by tiny shrimps, called cleaner shrimps. The huge eel could easily eat the shrimps, but it stays quite still while they pick dead **scales**, fungus, and bits of leftover food from its skin and sharp teeth.

cleaner shrimp

BARKO'S BLOG-TASTIC CORAL REEF FACTS

A clown fish lives among the stinging **tentacles** of a sea anemone. This keeps it safe from enemies. The fish does not get stung because its body is covered in special slime.

Slugs and Shells

Posted by: Ben Blog | January 14 at 1:24 p.m.

As I was heading back up to the boat, I spotted this super-sized shell. It's a giant clam, the biggest seashell in the world! It can measure more than 3 feet (1 meter) across and weigh more than 500 pounds (227 kilograms). The blue color on its lips is caused by tiny **algae**.

BARKO'S BLOG-TASTIC CORAL REEF FACTS
On land, slugs are plain brown or black, but sea slugs, like this Spanish dancer, have amazing colors, frills, and pointed **tentacles**. Their colors are a warning that they are poisonous!

Remarkable Reef

Posted by: Ben Blog | February 12 at 4:01 p.m.

The last stop on our trip was the Great Barrier Reef in Australia— the world's largest **coral reef**. It's home to thousands of astonishing animals, including 1,500 types of fish, 400 types of **coral**, 4,000 types of **mollusks,** and some rare **reptiles**, like this loggerhead turtle.

BARKO'S BLOG-TASTIC CORAL REEF FACTS

The Great Barrier Reef is more than 1,250 miles (2,000 kilometers) long. It's made up of thousands of smaller reefs and hundreds of tiny islands. It's so huge that it can be seen from outer space.

Coral Catastrophe

Posted by: Ben Blog | February 13 at 8:15 a.m.

All over the world, **coral reefs** are in danger. They are being damaged by **pollution**, shell and coral collectors, and companies drilling for oil. Huge patches of coral are turning white and dying. This is called coral **bleaching**. It happens when the ocean gets too salty or warm.

BARKO'S BLOG-TASTIC CORAL REEF FACTS
This odd-looking creature is a crown-of-thorns starfish. They have up to 20 arms and are covered in thick spines. They have eaten and killed enormous chunks of the Great Barrier Reef.

Remarkable Coral Reefs Quiz

If you are planning your own **coral reef** expedition, you need to be prepared. Find out how much you know about remarkable reefs with our quick quiz.

1. Which creatures build coral reefs?
a) reef sharks
b) coral **polyps**
c) sea anemones

2. What color is dead **coral**?
a) white
b) black
c) purple

3. Which fish have two spines on their tail?
a) lionfish
b) butterfly fish
c) surgeonfish

4. Where does a clown fish live?
a) in a hole in the coral
b) in a sea anemone
c) in a giant clam

5. How big is a giant clam?
a) 3 feet across
b) 30 feet across
c) 300 feet across

6. Where is the world's biggest reef?
a) India
b) Australia
c) Egypt

7. What is this?

8. What is this?

Glossary

algae tiny plant-like living thing

bleaching turning white

coral rock-like material made by tiny sea creatures

coral reef long structure made from coral that grows along the coast

habitat place where animals and plants live

inquisitive interested in learning about the world

Marco Polo explorer who lived from about 1254 to 1324. He traveled from Italy to China.

mollusk animal, such as a slug, snail, clam, or mussel

pollution things that make a place dirty or damage it, such as litter, oil, and chemicals

polyp tiny sea creature that makes coral reefs

predator animal that hunts and kills other animals for food

reptile cold-blooded animal that has scaly skin and lays eggs on land. Reptiles include snakes and lizards.

scale tiny flap covering a fish's body

school large group of fish, swimming together

tentacle long, waving body part that some sea creatures use to catch food

tropical found in warm parts of the world

Find Out More

Books

Ganeri, Anita. *Ocean Divers.* Chicago: Raintree, 2012.

Llewellyn, Claire. *Oceans (Habitat Survival).* Chicago: Raintree, 2013.

Murphy, Julie. *Ocean Animal Adaptations.* Mankato, Minn.: Capstone, 2012.

Salas, Laura Purdie. *Coral Reefs: Colorful Underwater Habitats.* Mankato, Minn.: Picture Window, 2009.

Web Sites

FactHound offers a safe, fun way to find Internet sites related to this book. All of the sites on FactHound have been researched by our staff.

Here's all you do:
Visit www.facthound.com
Type in this code: 9781432987800

Index